# FIGHTING FLAMES

Written by Keighley Douglas
Illustrated by Sawyer Cloud

## Contents

**OXFORD**
UNIVERSITY PRESS

# Words to look out for ...

**assist** *VERB*
To assist someone is to help them, usually in a practical way.

**essential** *ADJECTIVE*
Something that is essential is very important or absolutely necessary.

**manage** *VERB*
A person manages something when they control it or use it well.

**organize** *VERB*
When you organize something, you plan it and arrange it.

**routine** *NOUN*
a regular or fixed way of doing things

**sense** *NOUN*
an idea of what something is like

# The fire service

Day or night, the fire service is ready to <u>assist</u> us whenever we need it. Firefighters use special kit and **technology** to put out fires and keep us safe.

How did the fire service become what it is today? How did people fight fires in the past? To find out, we need to go back thousands of years. Let's go!

---

To <u>assist</u> someone is to help them, usually in a practical way.

# The first fire pump

People have been firefighting since ancient times. For a long time, people used buckets of water to put out fires.

More than 2000 years ago, a Greek-Egyptian inventor called Ctesibius (say: *tuh-sib-ee-us*) created the first **fire extinguisher** to put out a fire. He invented a pump that could squirt large jets of water from a well.

a water pump

# Ancient firefighting

2000 years ago in the city of Rome, fires often broke out. The **Roman emperor** Augustus realized that it was <u>essential</u> to have a group of people who would put out fires. Today we call these people the fire brigade.

At the time, the city had watchmen: a group of men who kept order in the city. Augustus <u>organized</u> them into a special firefighting team.

The watchmen became known as the 'little bucket fellows'! Can you guess why?

Something that is <u>essential</u> is very important or absolutely necessary.

When you <u>organize</u> something, you plan it and arrange it.

To stop a fire from spreading, the watchmen used a variety of tools, such as axes and ladders.

The axes allowed them to pull down the burning parts of buildings. It is thought that they used ladders to reach fires on upper floors. They may have also used them to rescue people trapped inside.

# The Great Fire of Rome

When Emperor Nero ruled ancient Rome, over half of the city was destroyed by a fire.

In the end, the watchmen had to knock down whole buildings to stop the fire from spreading. This created big gaps between the buildings, so the fire didn't have anything to burn.

Nero

Some people thought that Nero started the fire on purpose, so he could build the city the way he wanted.

After the fire, people realized safety rules were needed. In the new city, there were more open spaces and wider streets. The gaps between buildings acted as **firebreaks**. The city's water supply system was also improved, which made it easier to put out fires quickly.

ruins of an ancient Roman **fire station**

# The Great Fire of London

In 1666, a fire broke out in London and spread quickly. Without a fire brigade, the city was unable to deal with such a large fire. The fire burned for five days.

Here is a section from the diary of Samuel Pepys, 1666. He kept a very detailed diary of his life.

"300 houses have been burned down to-night by the fire ... it is now burning down all Fish Street, by London Bridge."

Samuel Pepys

The fire spread quickly because:

🔥 Buildings were made from wood, which is highly **flammable**.

🔥 It had been a dry summer and there were strong winds which meant the fire spread faster.

🔥 The city had narrow streets, so the flames spread easily to other buildings.

🔥 The people in charge had no plan to handle this kind of emergency.

One way of firefighting was the use of fire buckets. Ordinary people would pass buckets of water to each other to put out the flames.

Another method was a small hand-held pump that could squirt a jet of water.

Neither of these tools could handle the fire of 1666. Thousands of people lost their homes. Most of London was destroyed in under five days!

water squirt

fire bucket

These objects are like the ones used during the Great Fire of London.

When London was built again after the fire, buildings were made from brick and stone to help stop them from catching fire again.

Streets were built wider to prevent a fire from spreading. Houses were not allowed to have too many floors. This stopped them from being too crowded.

Safety routines were also introduced. Fire wardens took care of their own neighbourhoods. Every town in Britain had to have firefighting kit available.

wider streets

This is one of the plans for building London again.

A routine is a regular or fixed way of doing things.

# Modern firefighting

In 1824, firefighter James Braidwood helped to create the first fire brigade for a whole city in Edinburgh, Scotland.

His brigade had new and better firefighting kit, such as fire engines and hoses. He also made sure firefighters had special training.

James Braidwood went on to be the first head of the London Fire Service.

a horse-drawn
fire engine in 1824

James Braidwood constantly improved firefighting methods and firefighter training. He was also interested in fire prevention and building safety.

Many of his ideas have shaped the fire service we have today.

a firefighter giving a safety talk

# Fire engines then and now

**1600s**

In the 1600s, fire engines looked very different! They were made up of a central barrel with a water pump.

**1800s**

By the mid-1800s, steam-powered fire engines were used a lot. They were pulled by horses.

**1900s**

In the early 1900s, petrol-powered fire engines appeared.

**Today**

Today, fire engines have a variety of tools, including hoses and ladders. Most ladders reach up to around 4 floors. Some can reach 15 floors.

# Firefighter uniforms

Firefighters' uniforms are designed to protect them from heat and flames. Breathing **apparatus** protects firefighters from smoke and dangerous fumes.

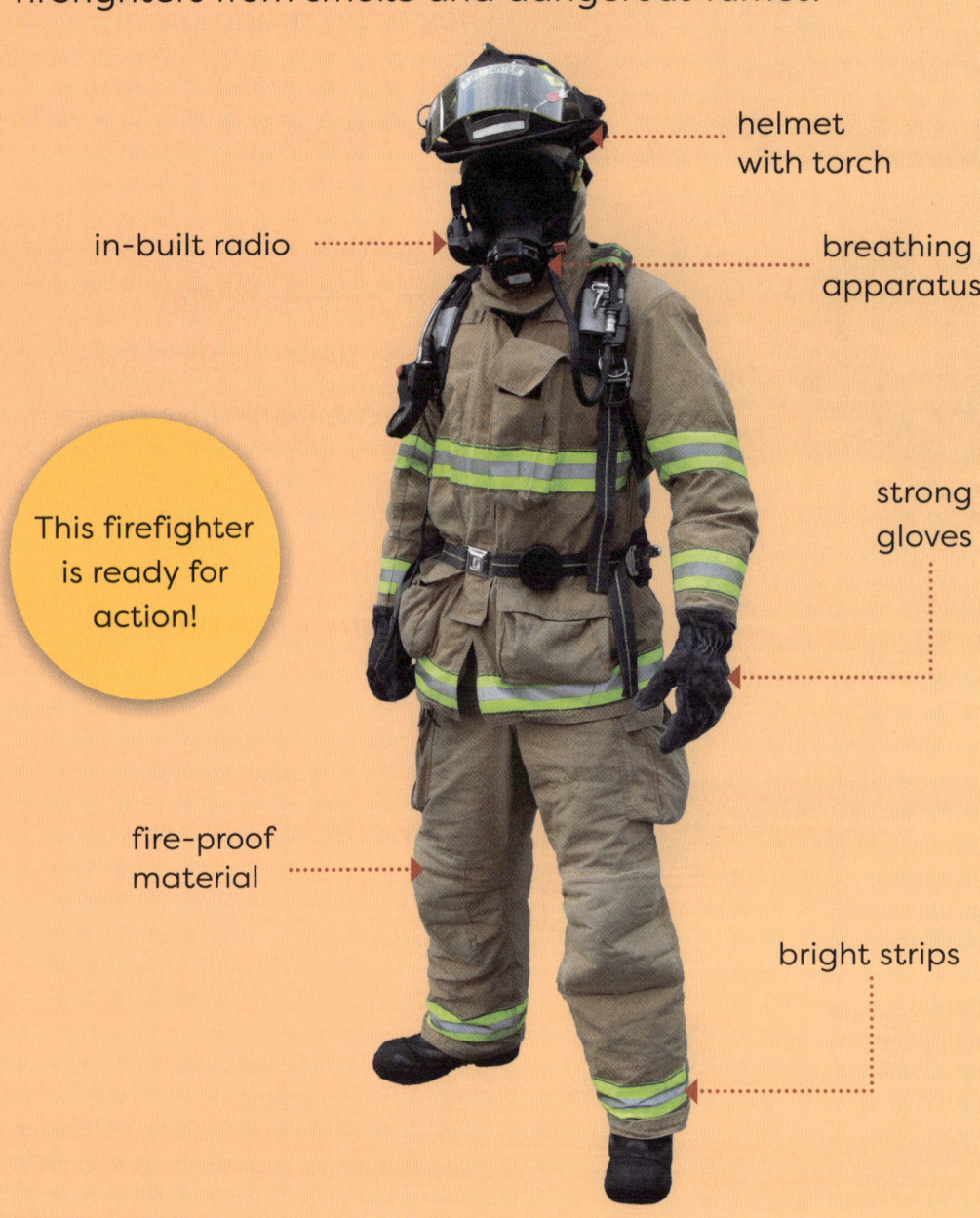

helmet
with torch

in-built radio

breathing
apparatus

strong
gloves

This firefighter
is ready for
action!

fire-proof
material

bright strips

# Firefighting today

Firefighters now have special technology to help them put out fires.

**Thermal** image cameras help firefighters see through thick smoke.

Drones with cameras give firefighters a <u>sense</u> of how big a blaze is.

Special technology can also predict the spread of a fire. This technology helps firefighters to make quick decisions.

---

To get a <u>sense</u> of something is to get an idea of what it is like.

Buildings have many things to keep us safe from fire. These include:

water sprinklers

emergency exits

smoke detectors and alarms

extinguishers

Places such as schools must also have a clear plan on how to get everyone out if there is a fire. Fire services work with building companies to make sure buildings are as safe as possible.

# Tackling wildfires

Wildfires are big fires that can happen in forests and grassy areas. As the **climate** changes, parts of the world are getting warmer and drier. This makes it easier for wildfires to start and spread.

**Indigenous** peoples have ways of firefighting that have been used for hundreds of years. They have a good understanding of how to <u>manage</u> the land.

Wildfires cause huge damage to homes and wildlife.

A person manages something when they control it or use it well

The Yurok and Karuk tribes of Northern California in the USA once practiced controlled burns. This is when fires are started on purpose to clear the land of dead plants. The cleared land also creates a firebreak, stopping fires from spreading.

The indigenous people in the Amazon rainforest have also used controlled burns for many years.

When carried out properly, controlled burns can protect against wildfires and the firebreaks can help certain useful plants to grow.

Modern firefighters carefully carrying out a controlled burn in the USA.

# Women in the fire service

For a long time, women were not allowed to become firefighters. People thought women couldn't do dangerous, physical jobs.

During World War I, many men who were firefighters had to join the army. To replace them, a fire brigade of women was formed.

The brigade was a great success. It started to change people's opinions about women in the fire service.

a Ladies Fire Brigade, 1916

Today, more and more women are becoming firefighters all over the world.

Sue Batten became the first full-time female firefighter in the UK, in 1982.

Rosemary R. Cloud was the first Black woman to become a Fire Chief in the US, in 2002.

Harshini Kanhekar was the first woman to become a firefighter in India, in 2006.

# Training firefighters

It can take around six months to two years to train as a firefighter. Trainees practise how to put out fires in a range of different situations.

They also learn first aid and how to respond to other types of emergencies, like floods. They must keep very fit.

Firefighters need to be brave and work well in a team. Would you like to be a firefighter one day?

# Glossary

**apparatus**: the equipment needed for an activity

**climate**: the usual kind of weather in a particular area

**firebreaks**: things that block or stop a fire from spreading

**fire extinguisher**: a device that is used to put out fires

**fire station**: a base for firefighters and the building where kit and fire engines are kept

**flammable**: able to catch fire quickly and easily

**indigenous**: people, plants and animals that have existed in a land since the earliest times

**Roman emperor**: the person in charge of the Roman Empire, which controlled lots of countries 2000 years ago

**technology:** tools, machines and equipment that help carry out tasks

**thermal**: energy produced by heat

# Index